Sam can run.
Run fast Sam.

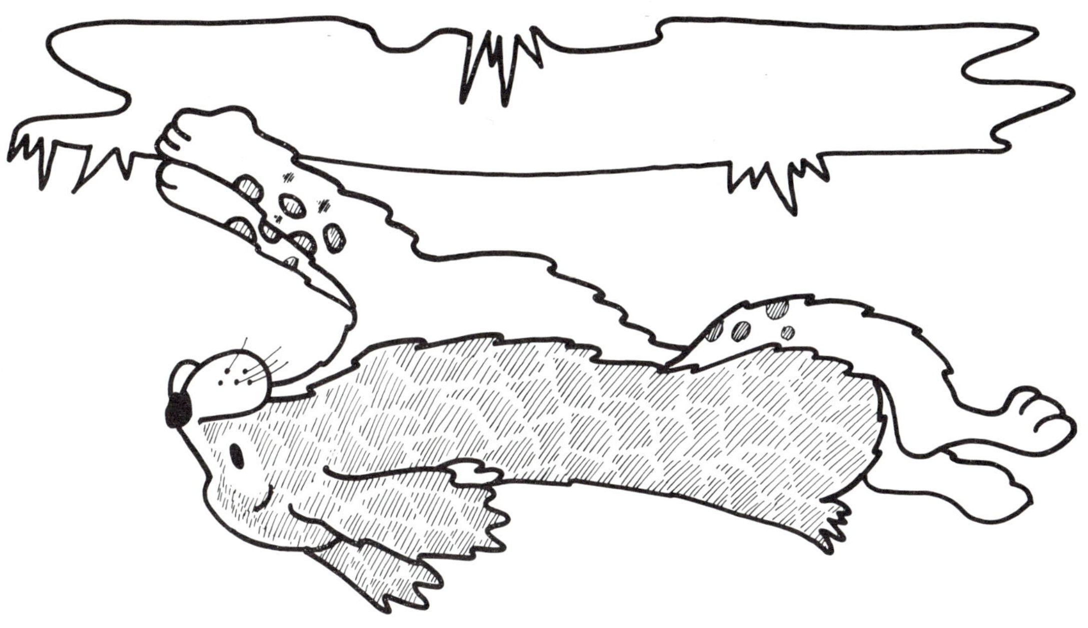

Sam

Sam is a dog.

Sam can wag.

Wag, Sam, wag.

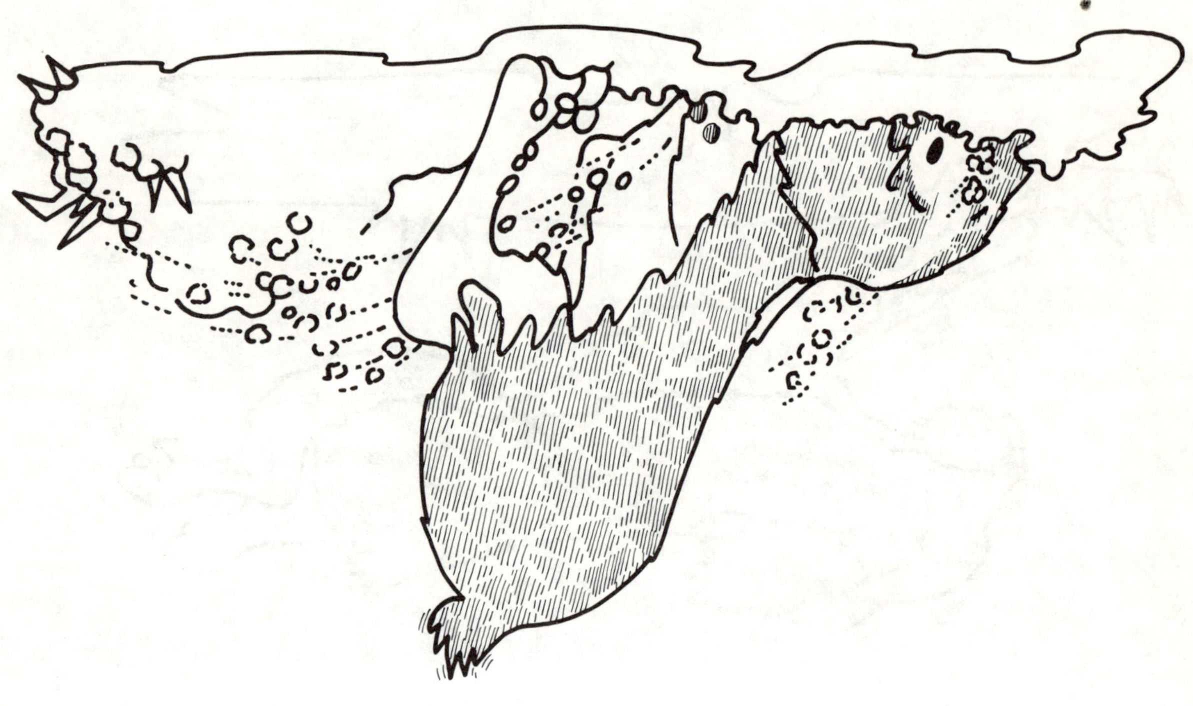

Sam can dig.

Bad dog, Sam.

© 1987 by EVAN-MOOR CORP.

Bob

Bob has a shop.
It is a fix-it shop.

A box is in the shop.
The box has a dent.

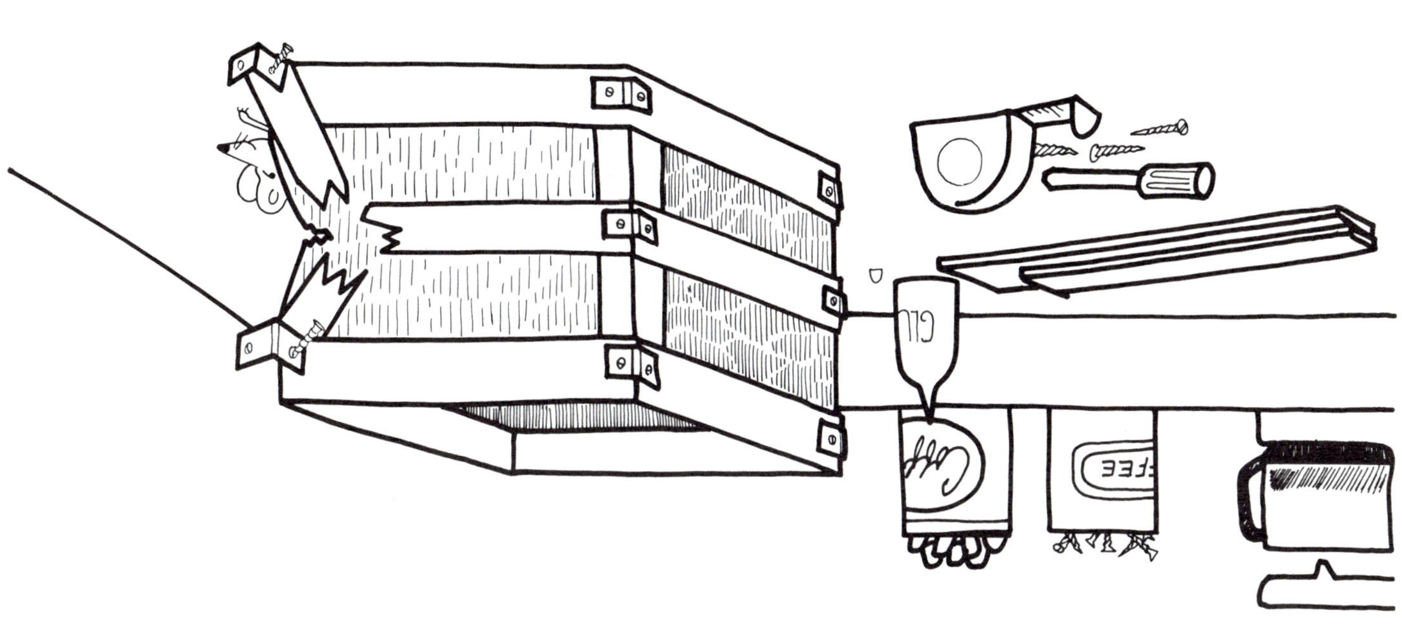

Bob did fix the box.

Can Bob fix it?
Can Bob fix the dent?

Bob and Sam

Bob has a pet.
The pet is Sam.
Bob went up the hill.
Sam went up the hill.

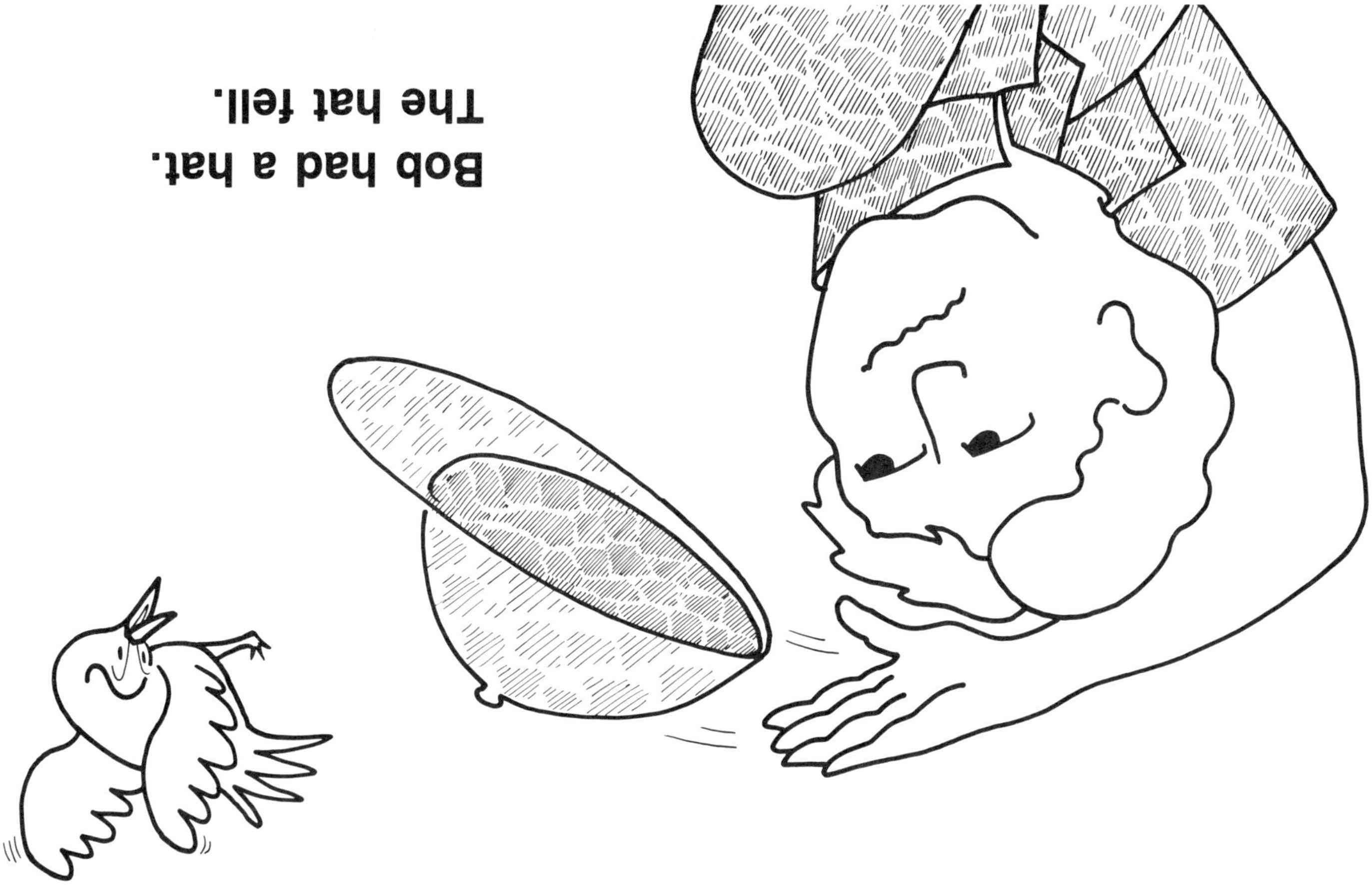

Bob had a hat.
The hat fell.

Sam got the hat.
Bob pets Sam.

Run, Sam, run.
Get the hat.
Will Sam get the hat?

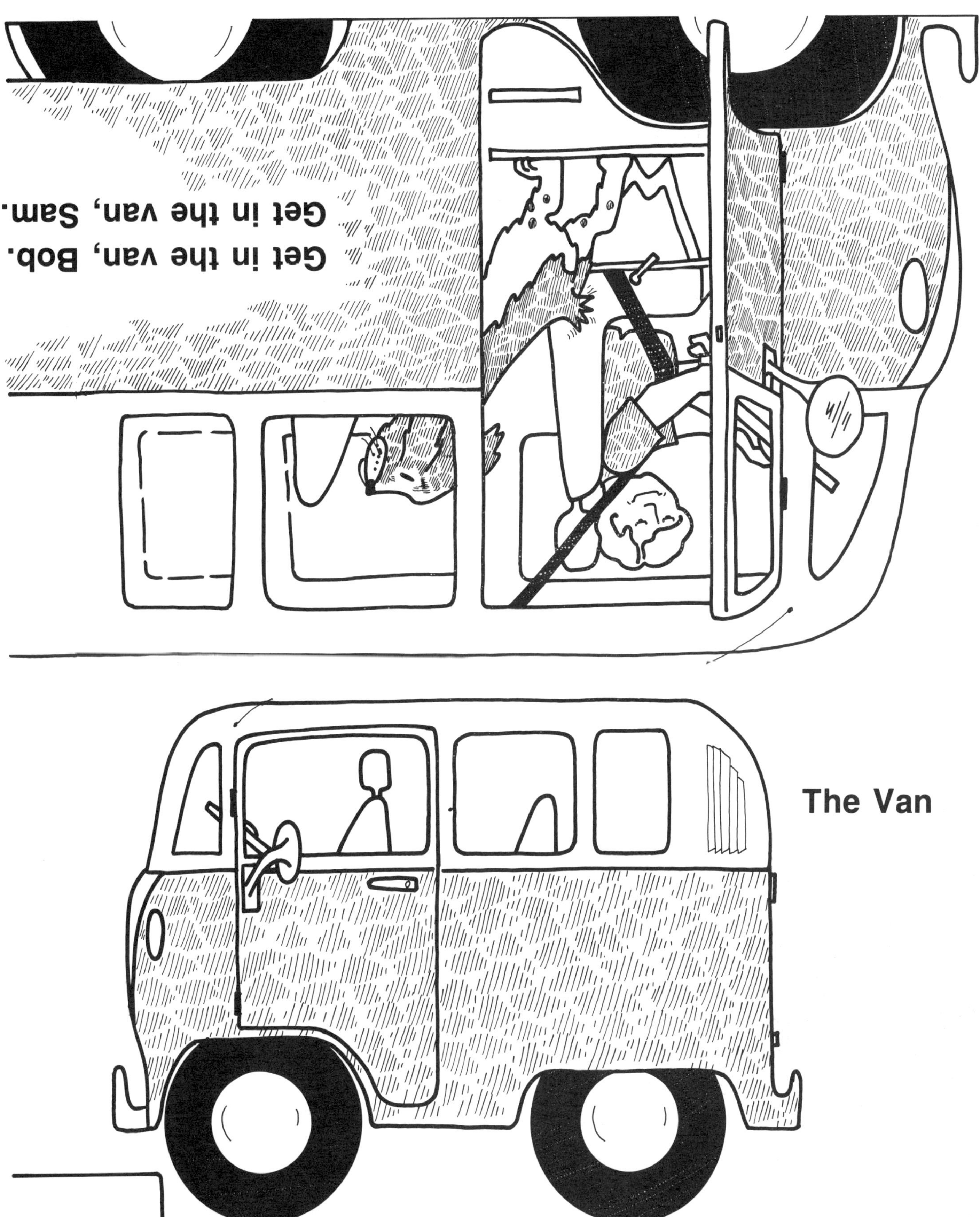

Get in the van, Bob.
Get in the van, Sam.

The Van

Bob has a van.
The van is big and red.

Go, Bob. Go, Sam.
It is fun to go in the van.

The van can go up a hill.
The van can go fast.

At The Pond

The pond is big.
A log is in the pond.
A frog is on the log.

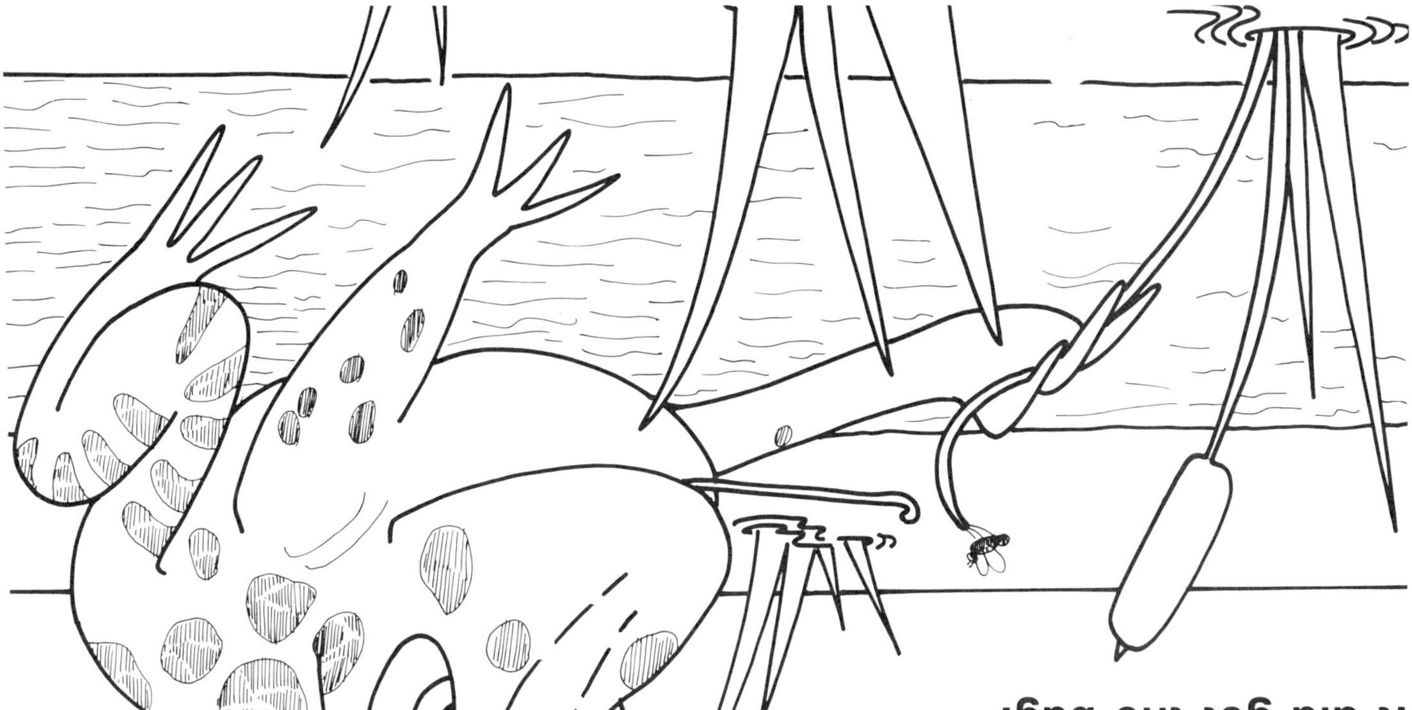

The frog can see a bug.
Can the frog get the bug?
It did get the bug.

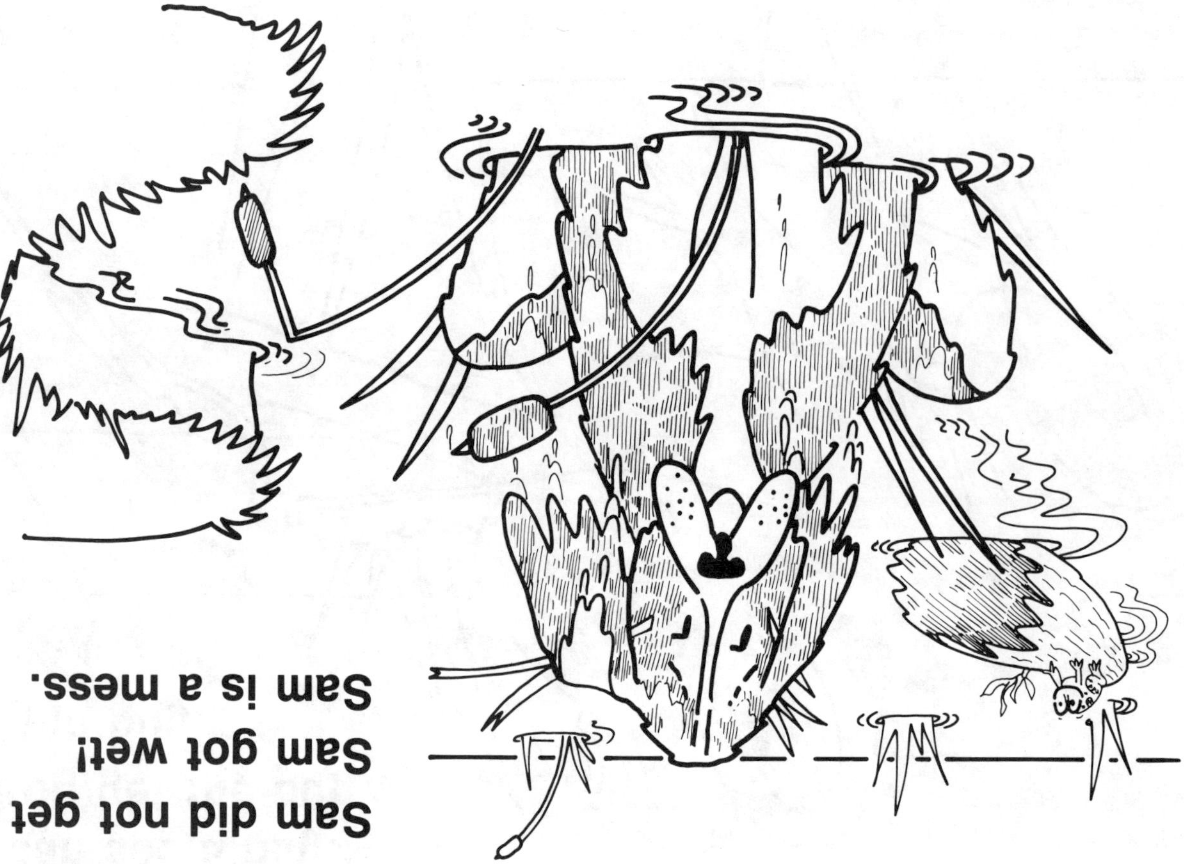

Sam runs to the pond.
Sam can see the frog.
Can Sam get the frog?

Sam did not get the frog.
Sam got wet!
Sam is a mess.

A Bone For Sam

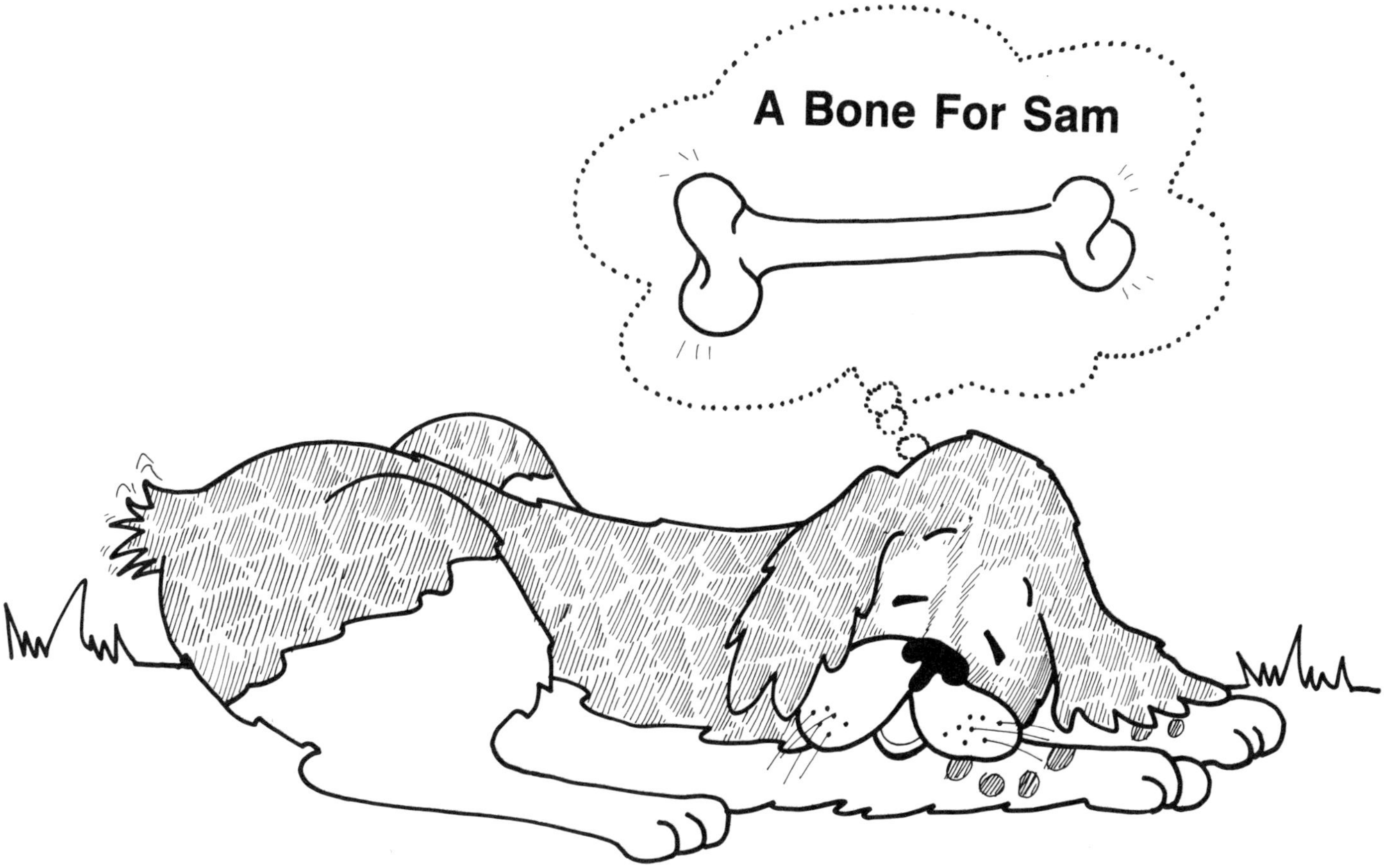

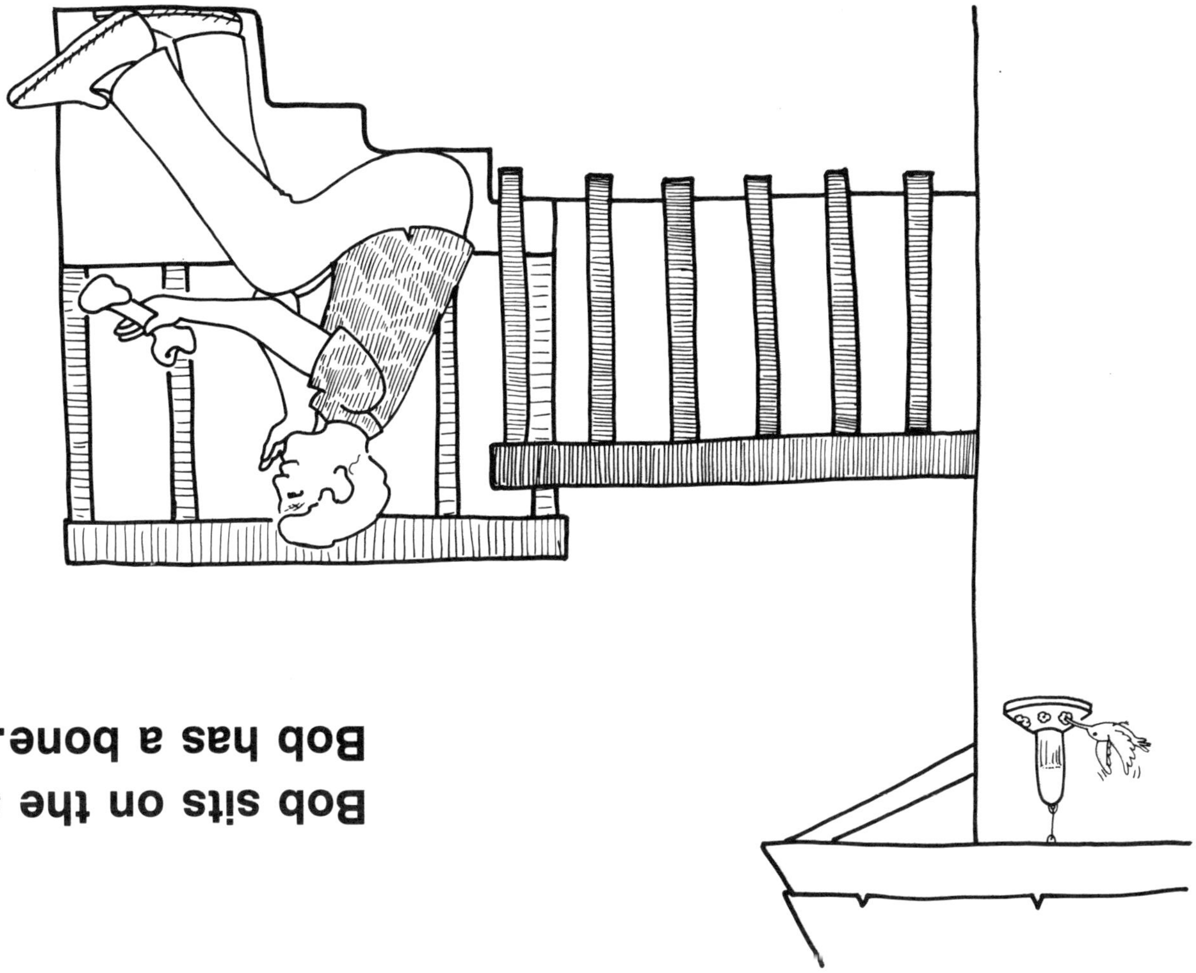

Bob sits on the step.
Bob has a bone.

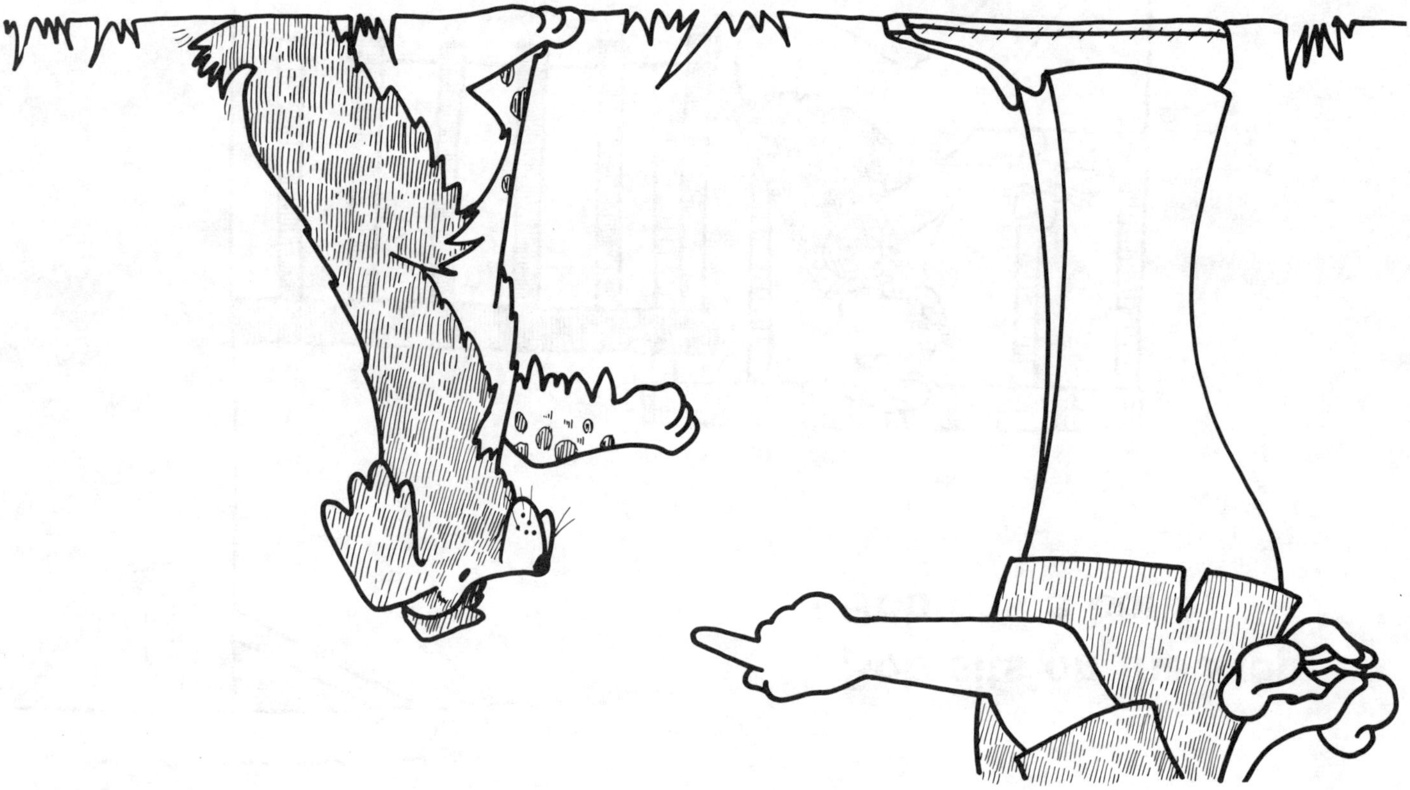

Sam runs to Bob.
Will Sam get the bone?

Sit, Sam, sit.
Sam must sit to get the bone.

Bob set the bone on Sam's paw.
Sit, Sam, sit.
Do not get the bone.

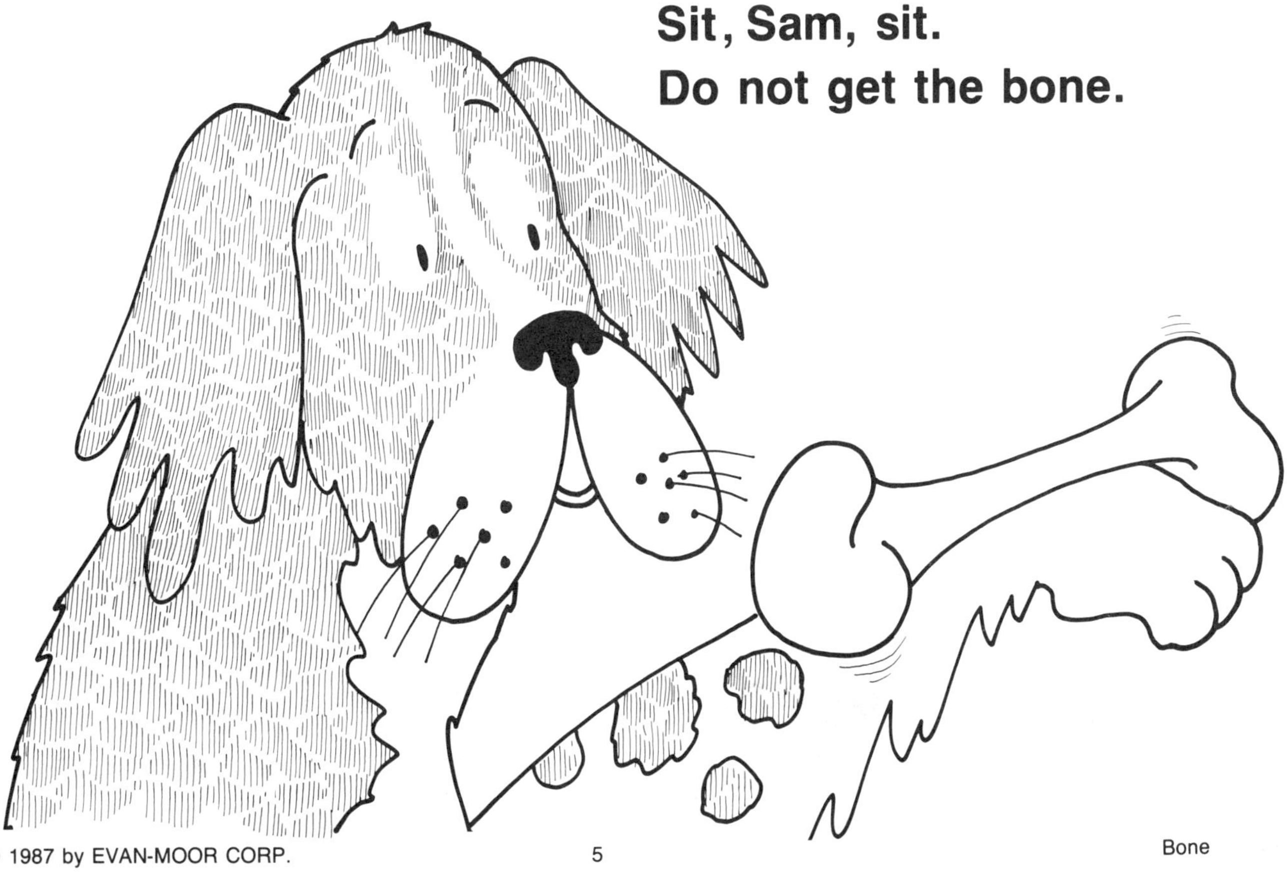

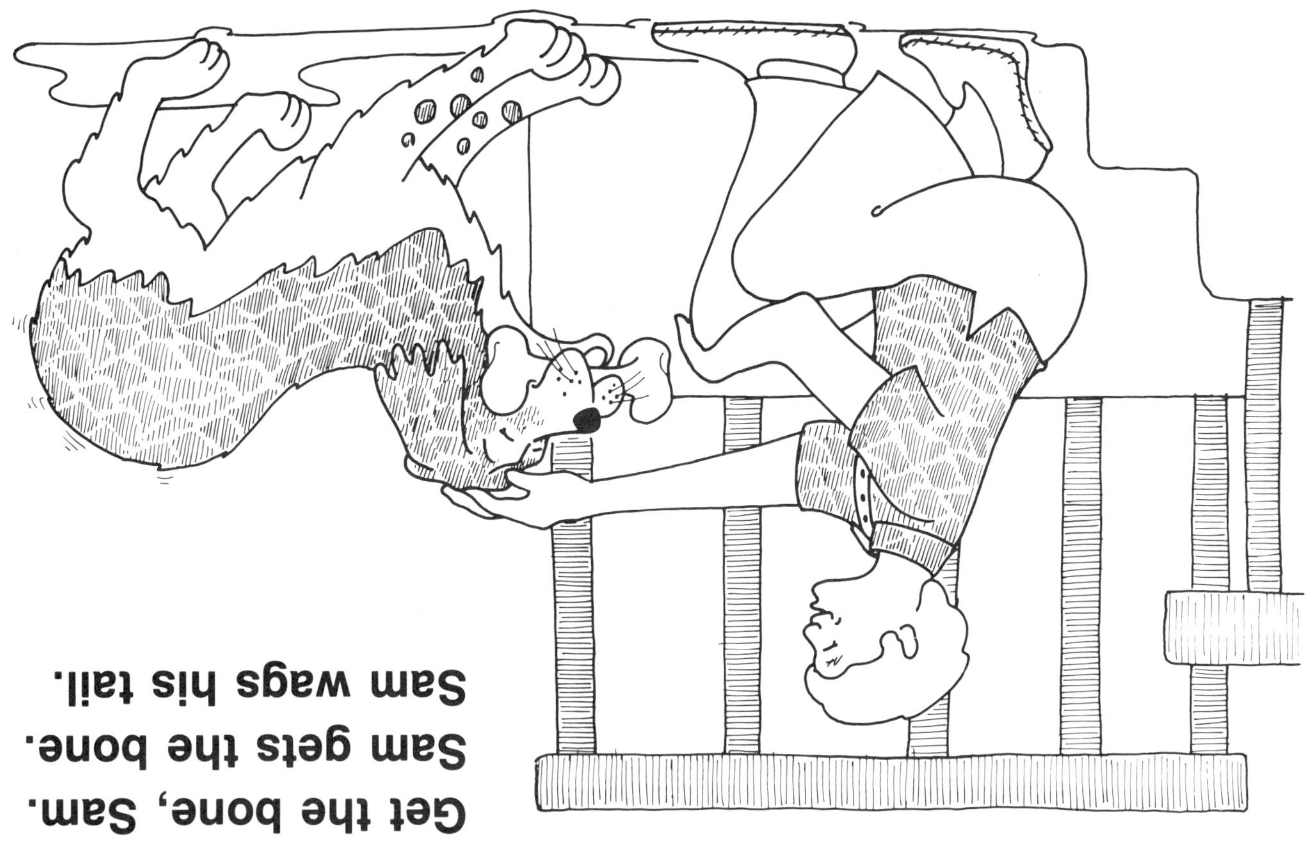

Get the bone, Sam.
Sam gets the bone.
Sam wags his tail.

Bob Helps

Les had to land.
He will get Bob to help.

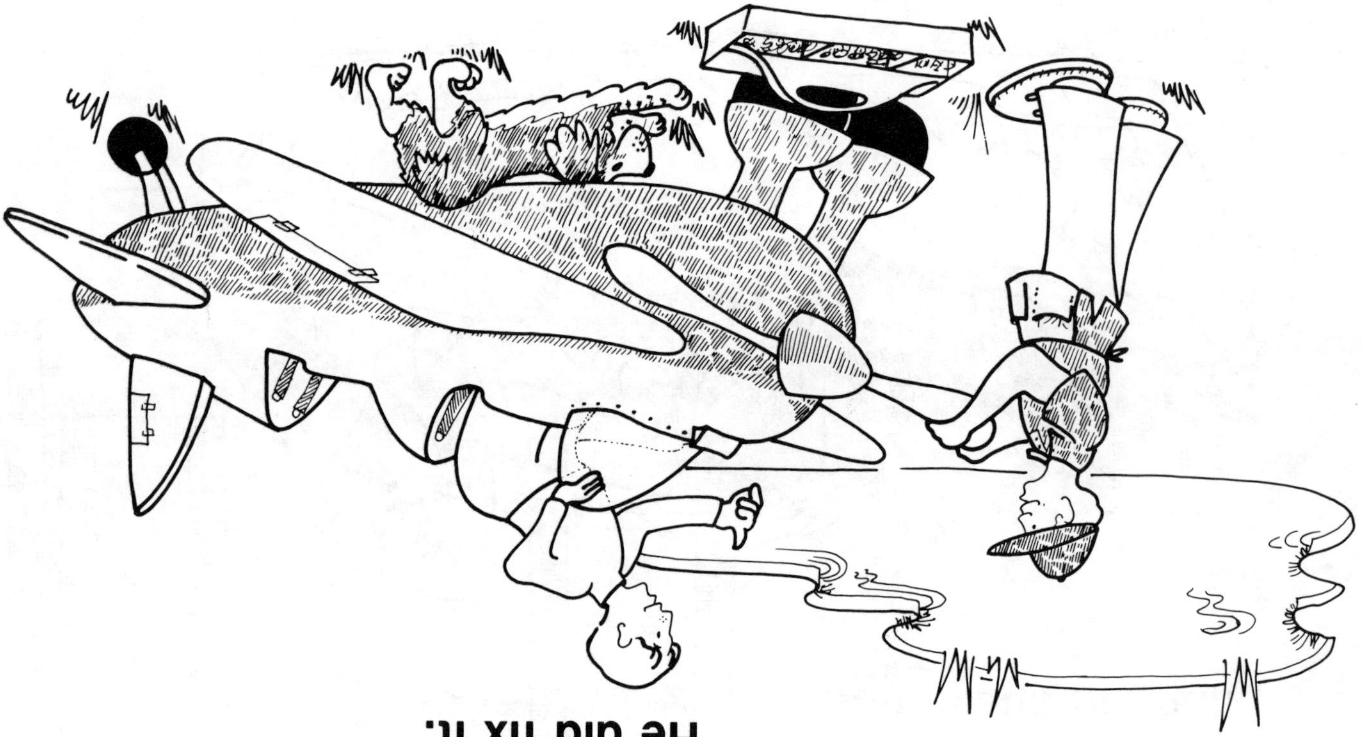

Bob and Sam go to the pond.
Bob can help.
He did fix it.

Bob is glad.
He can go up, up, up.

Sam is sad.
He can not go.

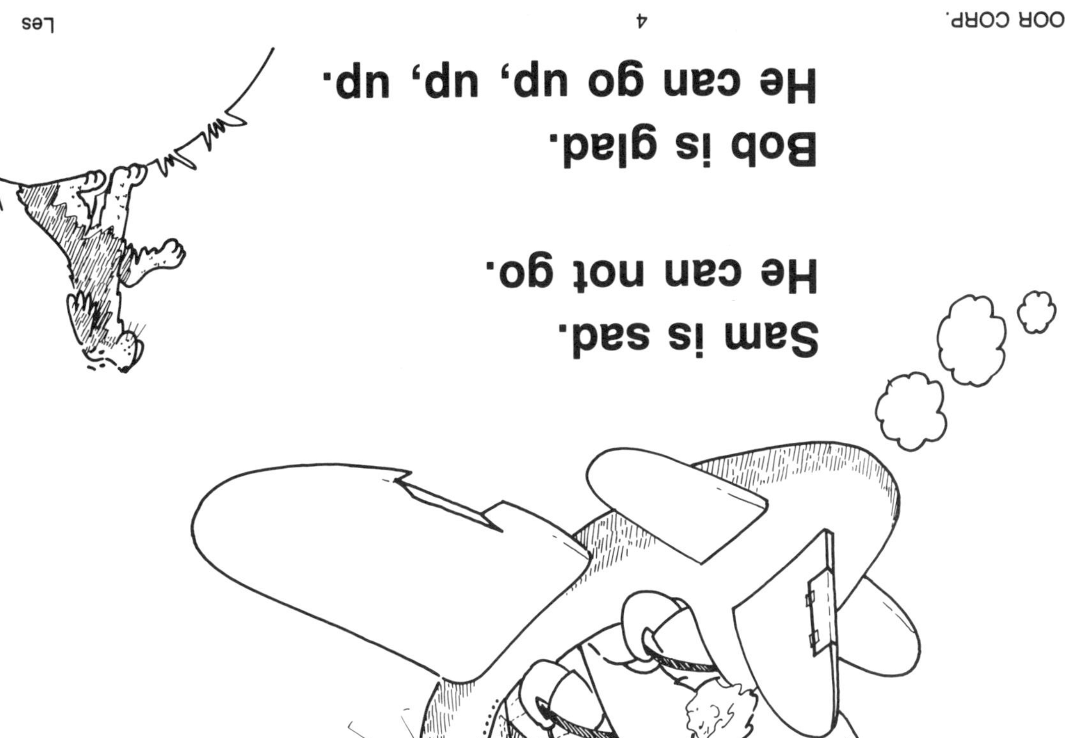

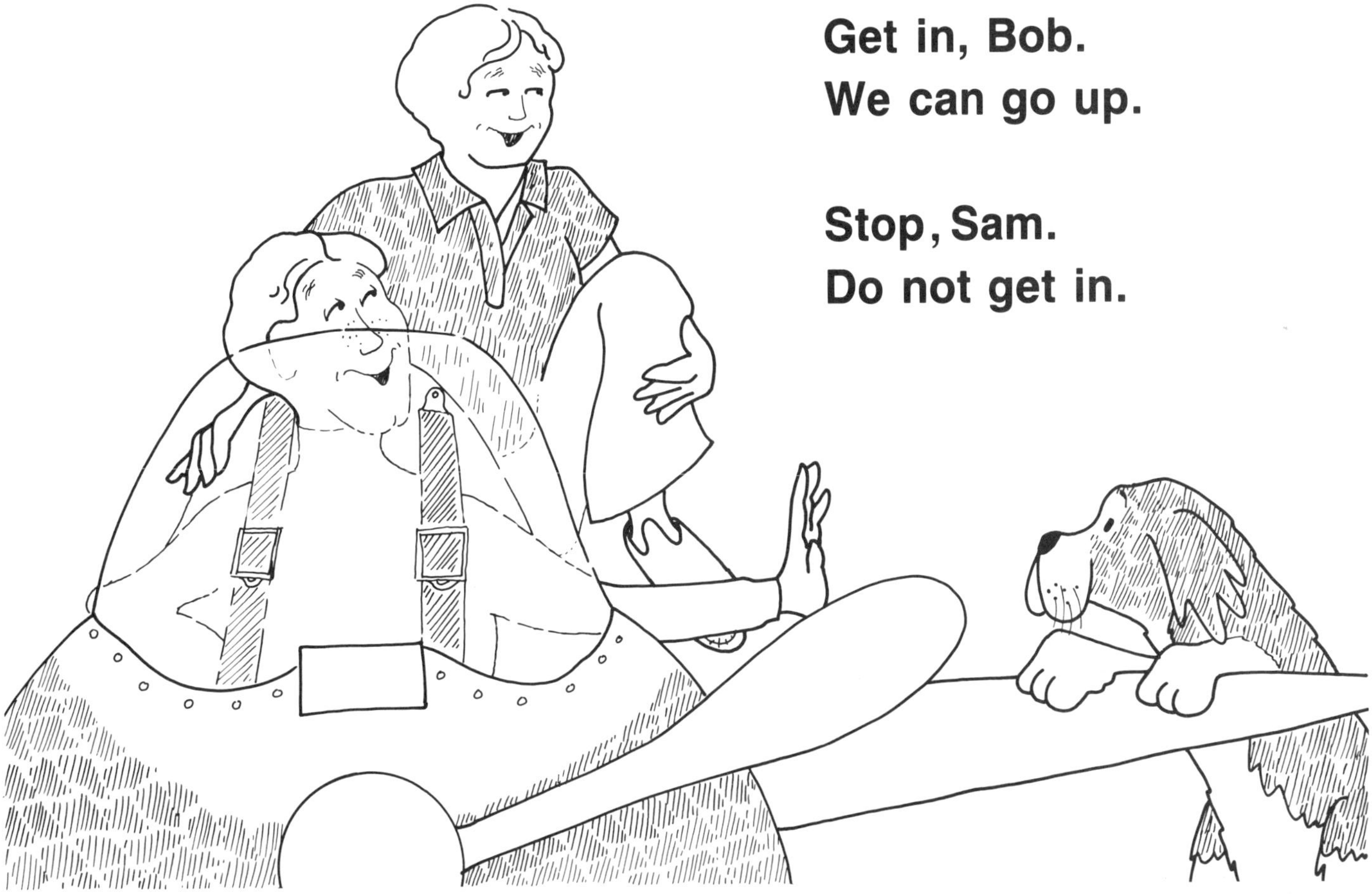

Get in, Bob.
We can go up.

Stop, Sam.
Do not get in.

The Bath

Sam ran and ran.
He got wet.

Sam dug in the mud.
He had fun.

Pam sees Sam in the mud.
Pam runs to get Bob.

Sam is a mess.
He must get a bath.

Bob got a tub.
Pam got a rag.
Get in the tub, Sam.

Sam did not get in the tub.
Sam ran and ran.

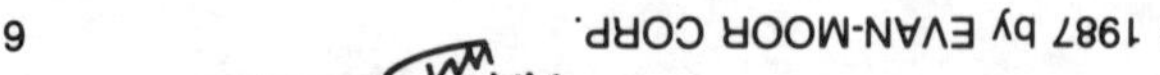

Bob ran fast.
Bob got Sam.

Sam is in the tub.
Sam will not be a mess.

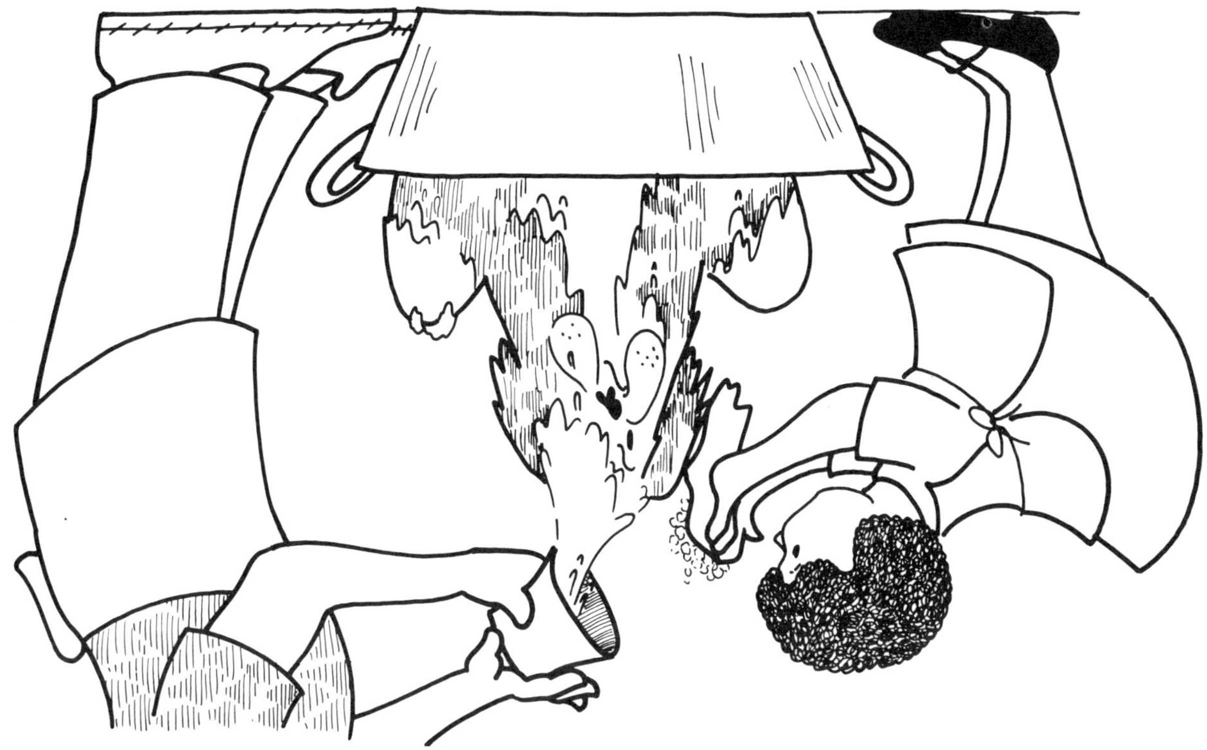

Camp

It is hot in the shop.
We can go in the van.
We can camp.

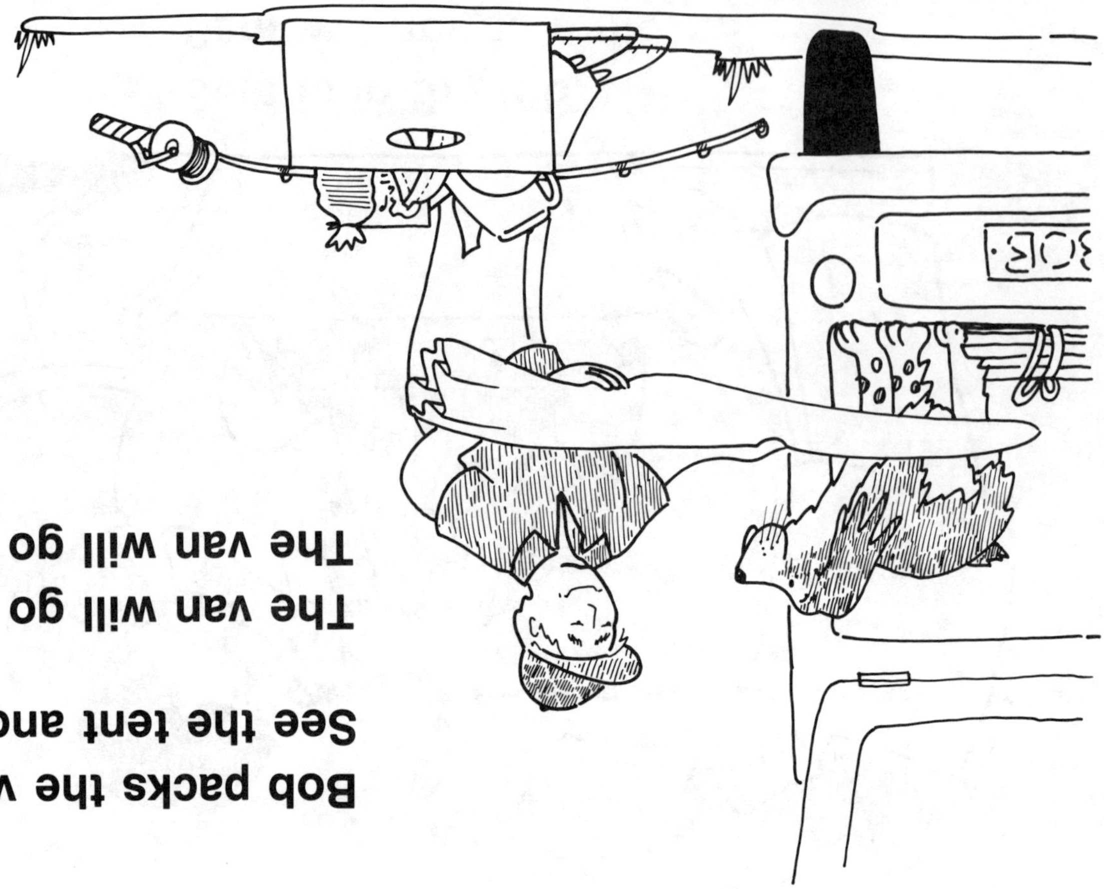

Bob packs the van.
See the tent and the box.

The van will go up the hill.
The van will go to the camp.

Bob and Sam run on the sand.
It is fun to camp.

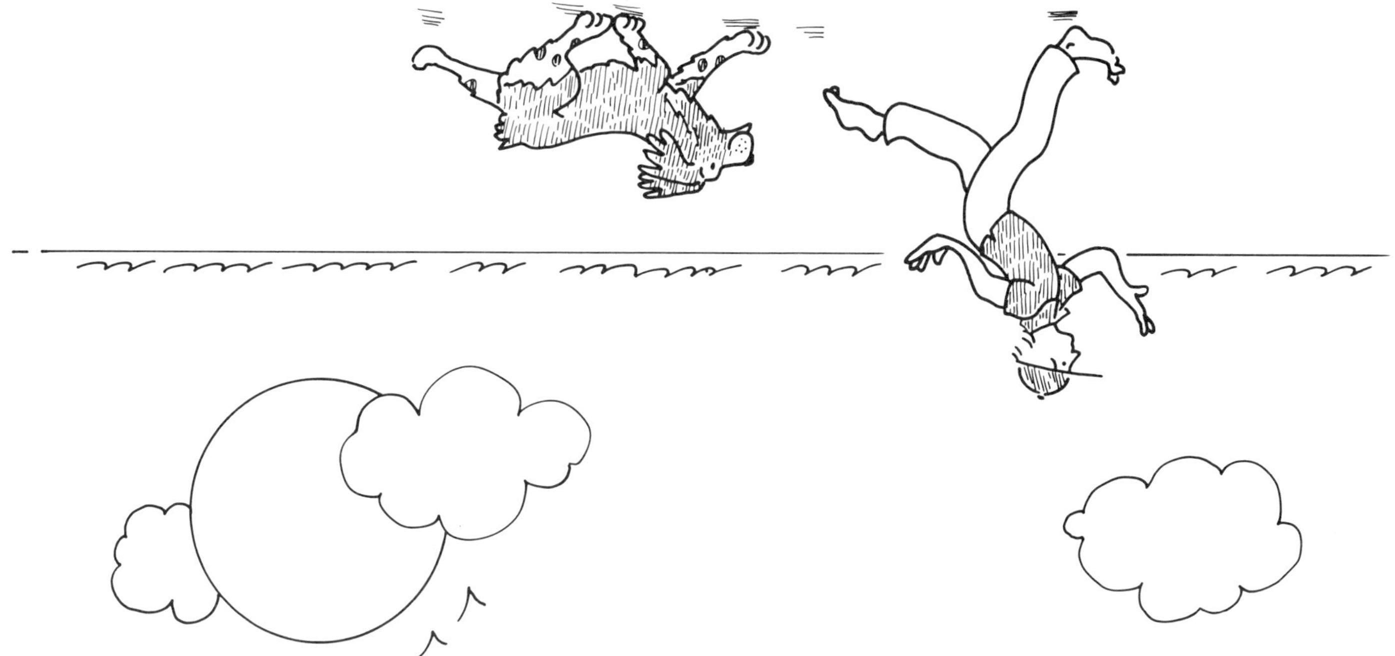

Bob set the tent on the sand.
Bob set the box in the tent.

Pam's Pet

Bob and Sam went to see Pam.
Bob had a box.
The box had a lid.

Bob set the box on the step.

Pam sees the box.
Pam can not see in it.

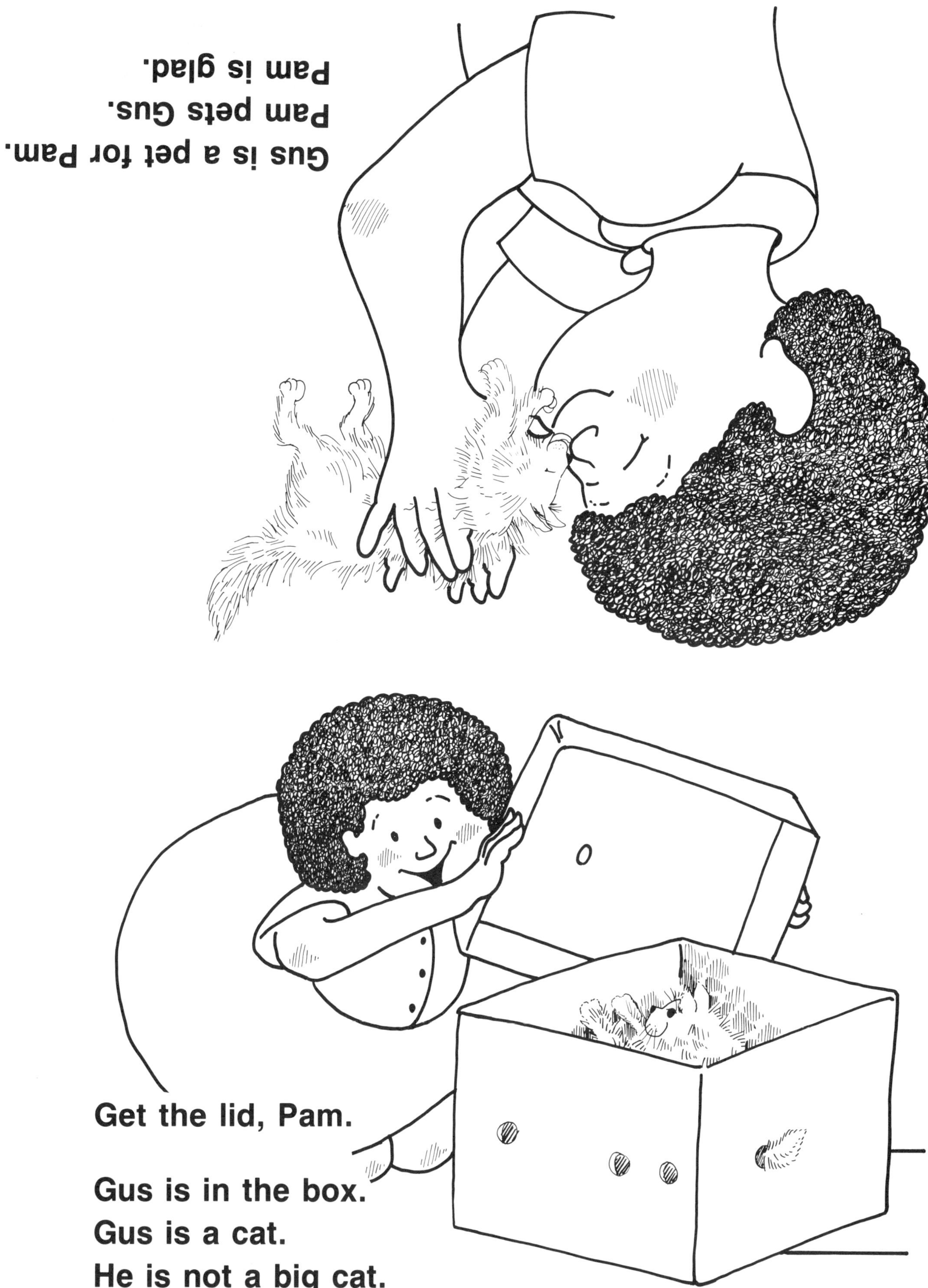

Get the lid, Pam.

Gus is in the box.
Gus is a cat.
He is not a big cat.

Gus is a pet for Pam.
Pam pets Gus.
Pam is glad.

Bob and Sam must go.
Pam hugs Bob.
Pam hugs Sam.

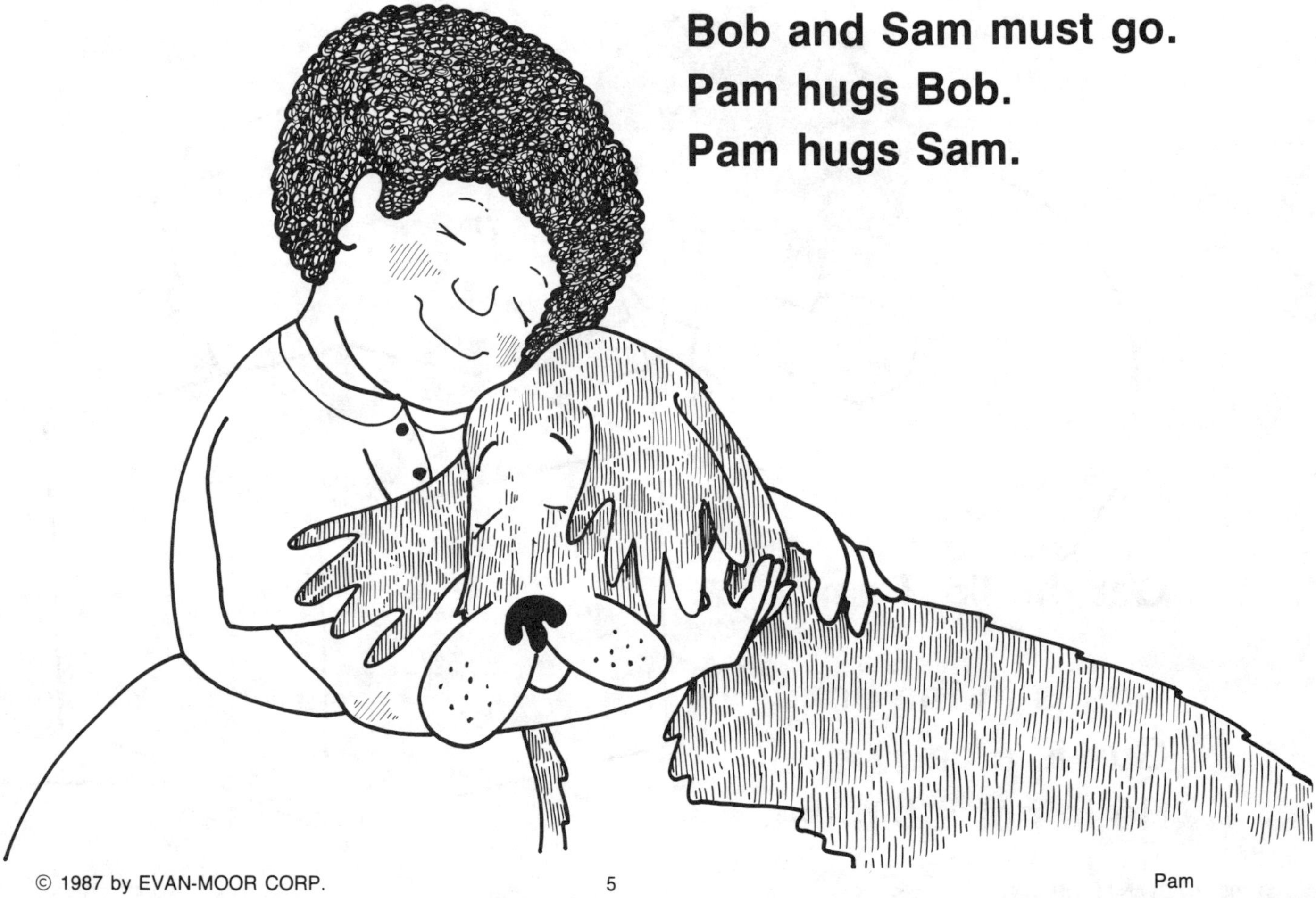

Pam and Gus sit on the step.
A pet cat is fun.

Sam's Trick

Bob and Sam go up the hill.
Bob has a stick.
He will toss the stick.

Run, Sam, run.
Run up the hill.
Get the stick.

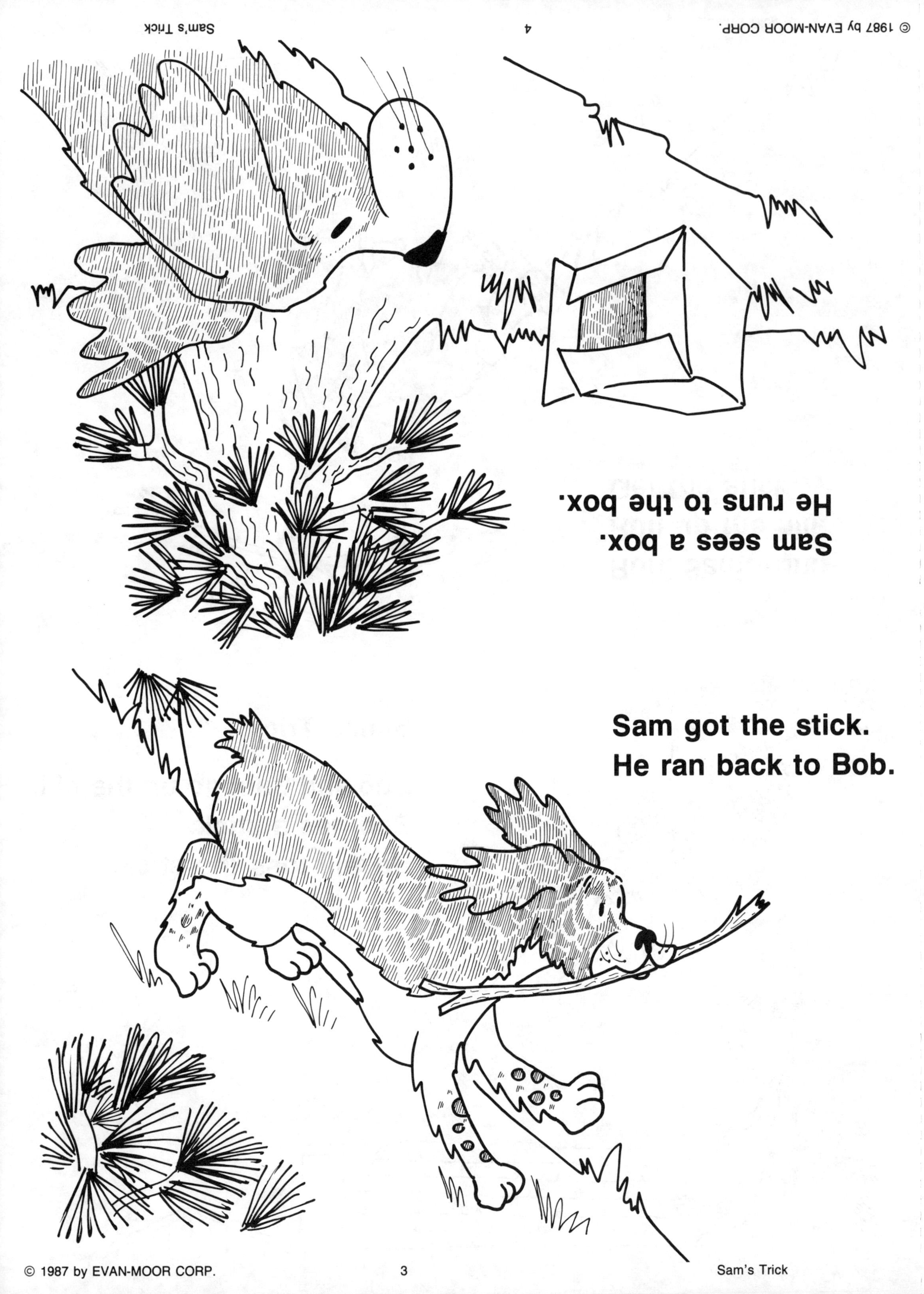

Sam sees a box.
He runs to the box.

Sam got the stick.
He ran back to Bob.

Bob helps Sam.
He gets the box off Sam.
Bob pets Sam.
Sam licks Bob.

Sam is stuck in the box.
Sam is sad.
He must get help.

Sam and Gus

Pam has a pig.
The pig can not go.
Pam must go to the fix-it shop.

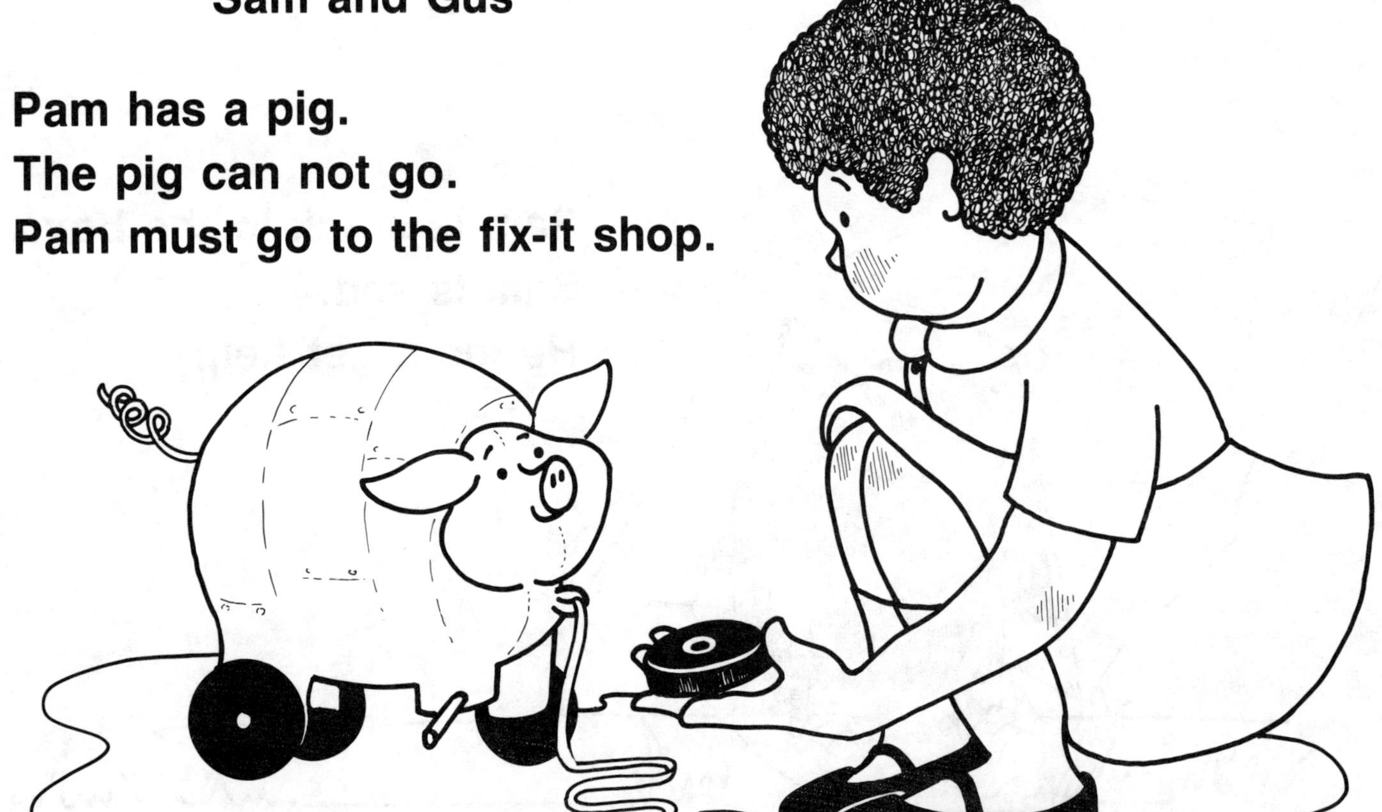

Pam went to see Bob.
Gus went to see Sam.

Gus sees Sam on the step.
Gus runs to Sam.
Gus and Sam go up the hill.

Bob can fix the pig.
He will fix it for Pam.
Pam can help Bob.

Pam had to go.
Pam got the pig.
Pam went to get Gus.

Pam did not see Gus and Sam.
Pam went to get Bob.
Can Bob get the pets?

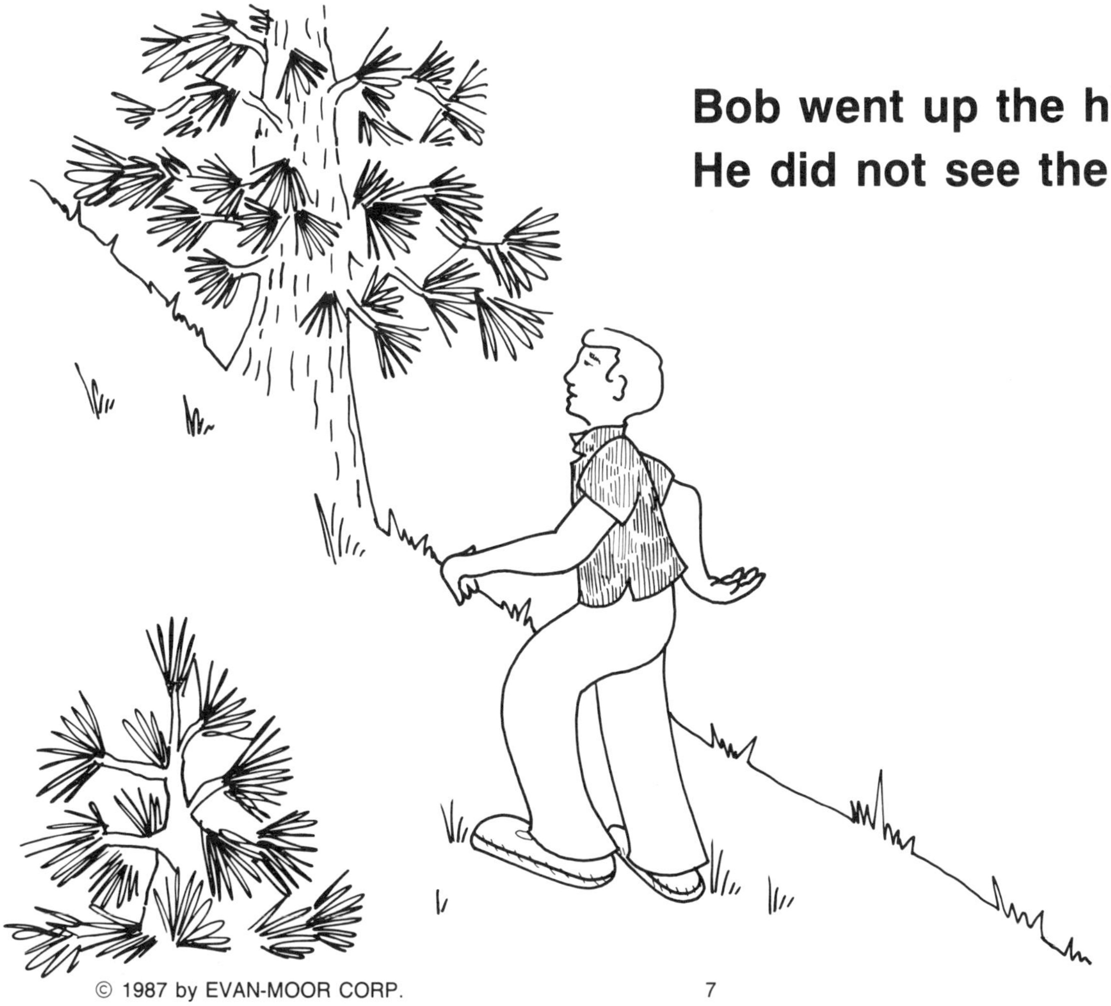

Bob went up the hill.
He did not see the pets.

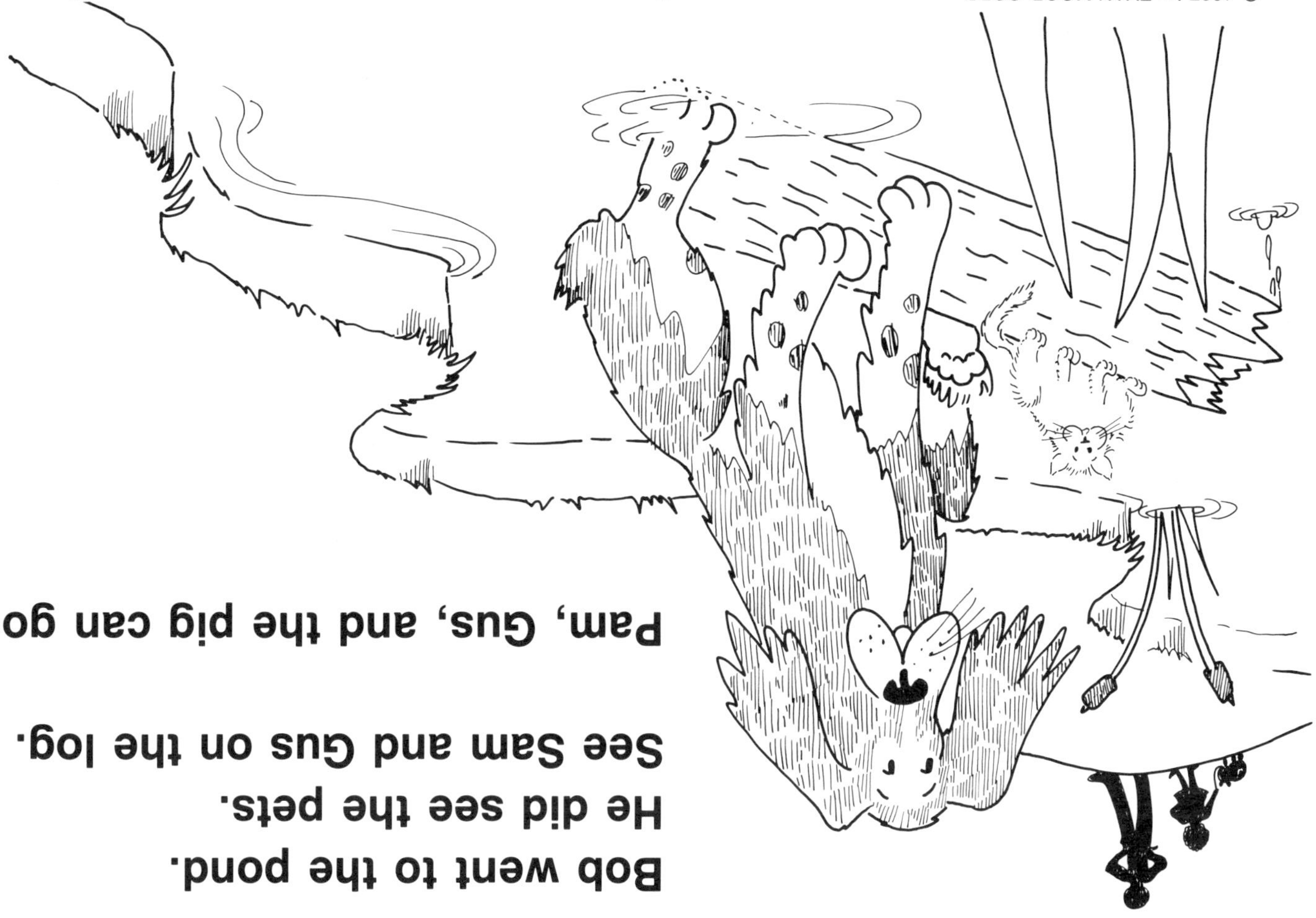

Bob went to the pond.
He did see the pets.
See Sam and Gus on the log.

Pam, Gus, and the pig can go.

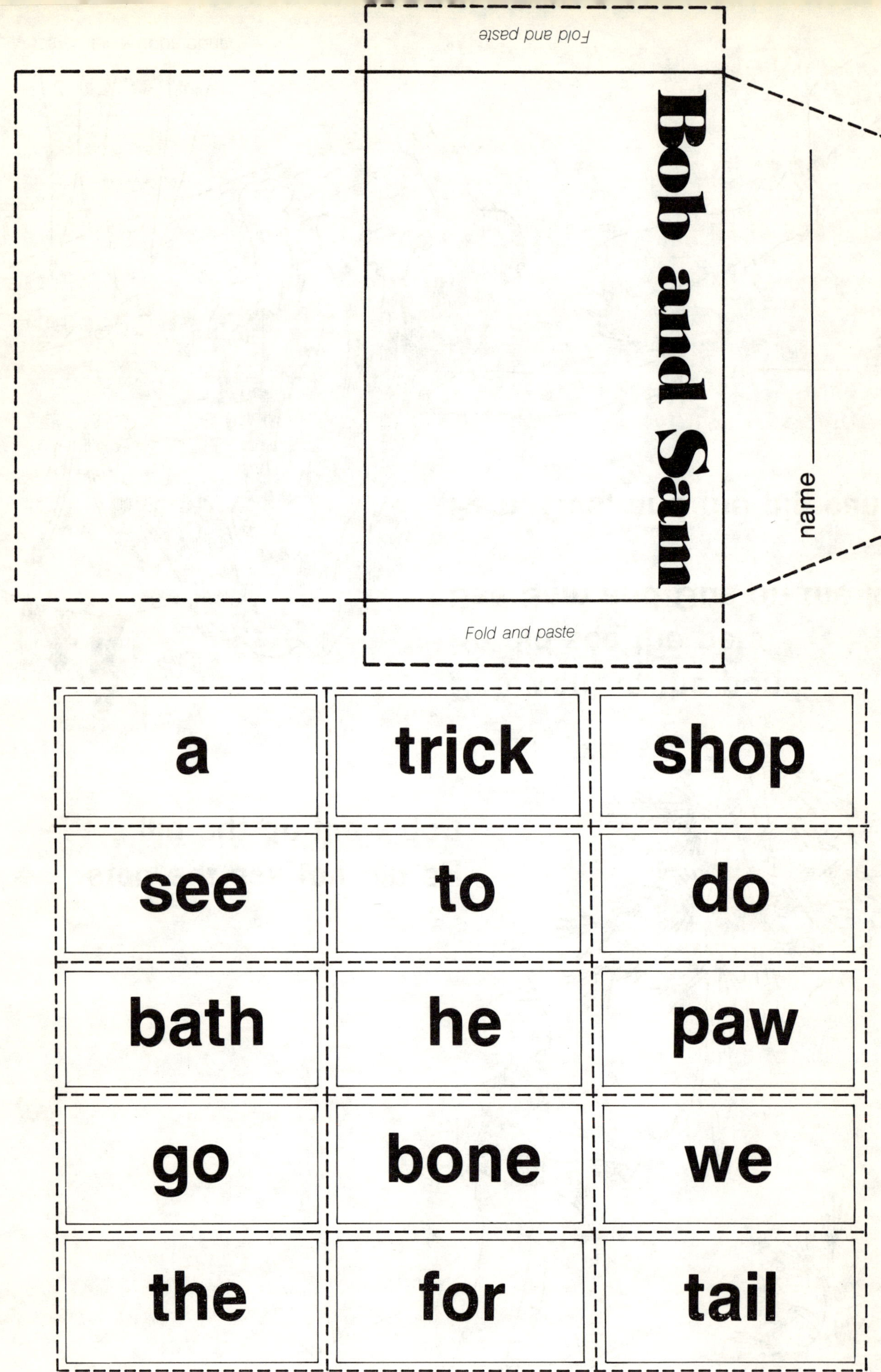
Fold and paste
Bob and Sam
name
Fold and paste
a
trick
shop
see
to
do
bath
he
paw
go
bone
we
the
for
tail